A Curator's

Introduction

to the

Camellia

Collection

in the

Huntington

Botanical

Gardens

THE HUNTINGTON LIBRARY
SAN MARINO & CALIFORNIA

Introducing the Huntington Botanical Gardens Camellia Collection

Railroad and real estate developer Henry Edwards Huntington (1850–1927) was a collector without equal who assembled world-class collections of rare books and manuscripts, works of art, and plants. Today his 206-acre estate near Los Angeles has fifteen theme gardens filled with twenty thousand different kinds of plants including 1,200 camellia cultivars and species. Huntington had a kindred spirit in his landscape gardener, William Hertrich, who took a special interest in the camellia collection.

With a blooming season from October to May, the camellias are a major attraction to visitors. This book offers general information about camellias so that a tour of the gardens might be more rewarding. For those who are interested in more information, a selective bibliography may be found at the end of the book.

© 2001 Henry E. Huntington Library and Art Gallery
1151 Oxford Road
San Marino, CA 91108
www.huntington.org
Printed in Singapore

This book is one of a series of publications on the Huntington Botanical Gardens made possible by a generous contribution from Helen and Peter Bing.

Design: Lilli Colton
Photographs by Don Normark, unless otherwise indicated;
Judi Danner, pages 9 (lower left), 15 (lower left), 17, 18, 19, 20, 21, 29, 35 (lower), 50, 53, 54, 59, 63;
Don Rogers, page 68 (top left)

COVER AND P. 2: 'Francie L.'
PAGE 3: 'Tiffany'

Library of Congress Cataloging-in-Publication Data

A curator's introduction to the camellia collection in the Huntington Botanical Gardens/Ann Richardson, [editor]. — rev. and expanded ed.
    p. cm. – (A Huntington pictorial guide)
  Original text by Amelia and Carey S. Bliss, with the assistance of Myron Kimnach. Current edition revised and expanded by Ann Richardson, Curator of the Huntington's Asian Gardens.
  Includes bibliographical references (p.).
  ISBN 0-87328-190-X (paper) – ISBN 0-87328-193-4 (cloth)
  1. Camellia. 2. Camellia—Varieties. I. Richardson, Ann, 1941 – II. Huntington Botanical Gardens. III. Series.

SB413.C18 C77 2001
635.9'33624—dc21   00-054689

Contents

Camellia sinensis,
*the tea plant, was
labeled* Thea viridis
*in this 1812
illustration from*
Curtis's Botanical
Magazine (#3148).
*All camellias belong
to the tea family,
the Theaceae.*

THE CAMELLIA'S LINEAGE is a distinguished one, beginning in Asia centuries ago, where such species as *Camellia oleifera* in China and *C. sasanqua* in Japan were grown for their oil-bearing seeds. *C. sinensis*, the tea plant, is another species whose origin is lost in dimmest antiquity. One legend has it that the custom of tea drinking began with Confucius as a means of persuading his followers to boil their water.

In time, some species came to be grown simply for the beauty of their blossoms; an ancient scroll indicates that *C. reticulata* was cultivated in China more than 900 years ago, probably as a sacred temple flower. Many soon found their way into private gardens, where they eventually attracted the attention of the early European explorers.

The camellia's generic name was assigned by the Father of Botany himself, Carl von Linné, or Linnaeus. He named it in honor of George Joseph Kamel, a Jesuit priest born in Moravia who did extensive botanical research in the Marianas and in the Philippines, where he died in 1706. Ironically, Kamel never visited China, and it is doubtful he ever saw the plant that bears his name.

The arrival of the first camellias in England came about as the result of an outright hoax, connected with the demand for tea. In the early eighteenth century, the Chinese had a virtual monopoly on tea culture, which sent prices soaring on the European market. Some of the British sea captains, logically enough, decided to try to import tea plants for cultivation in England, but the Chinese, not eager to lose this lucrative trade, substituted plants of the species *C. japonica* for the related *C. sinensis*. Although deprived of their tea, the English seem to have been quick in their appreciation of the substituted species, for by 1739, a red camellia was being raised in the greenhouses of Lord Petre at Thorndon Hall, his estate in Essex.

The Huntington has examples of the first named camellias introduced into the west, *C. japonica* 'Alba Plena' (a white formal double, still sold in nurseries today) and *C. japonica* 'Variegata' (a rare semidouble red variegated white), both of which arrived in England in 1792.

The first camellias came to America in 1797, where they were cultivated in Boston, New York, and Philadelphia greenhouses before their culture spread south and westward. Only three years after the Gold Rush started they were advertised for sale by a Sacramento, California, nurseryman and were soon quite common in the Sacramento-San Francisco area. Some of the oldest camellia plants in California still bloom on the state capitol grounds.

According to one source, the first camellia in Southern California was planted at Montecito, near Santa Barbara, in 1875. Records in the Los Angeles-San Gabriel Valley area show camellias in cultivation as early as 1888, the year that 'California' was introduced from Japan. When Huntington acquired his estate in 1903, two camellias were growing near the old James de Barth Shorb house, site of the present Huntington Art Gallery. One of these, 'Pink Perfection', still thrives in the garden north of the Art Gallery, along the path on the west side of the North Vista.

Of much later date, but deserving mention, was the start of a collection at Descanso Gardens in nearby La Canada. This land, the last acreage of the old Rancho San Rafael, was purchased in 1935 by the late Manchester Boddy, then publisher of the *Los Angeles Daily News*. He purchased a considerable number of camellias in 1941, and began research into cultivation and propagation.

'Alba Plena'

'Variegata'

'California'

'Pink Perfection'

'Lady MacKinnon'

The camellia collection got its real start in 1908 and 1909 when approximately two dozen good-sized plants were purchased from a local nursery. The second large acquisition of camellias came in 1913 with the development of the Japanese Garden. Plants, garden ornaments, and a traditional Japanese house were brought to the Huntington estate. In 1918, a small shipment of camellias was purchased directly from Japan and modest additions to the collection continued until World War II.

In 1942, the Friends of the Huntington Library became interested in augmenting the camellia collection. They allocated funds for acquiring new plants and by the end of that year 125 new cultivars had been added. The Southern California Camellia Society became interested in the project in 1944, and plans were formed to assemble and organize the collection as a distinctive feature of the Huntington Botanical Gardens.

The gardens boast approximately 1,200 cultivars and species of camellias, the total number of camellias being more than that, allowing for duplication. Additional cultivars are added as interesting introductions become available. The plants cover an area of more than fifteen acres, concentrating in two sections—the North Vista, directly north of the Huntington Art Gallery, and in the area north of the Japanese Garden, the North Canyon Camellia Garden. Species Lane, a newly landscaped` area behind the North Vista and east of the Scott Gallery, is planted with camellia species, those that grow naturally in the wild. (see MAP)

Although the climate of Southern California is generally favorable to the outdoor culture of camellias, certain precautions must be taken. All-day exposure to direct sunlight accompanied by low humidity presents a real danger to the plants. At the Huntington, the overhanging branches of shade trees give natural protection from the sun, and their fallen leaves provide a mulch that protects the camellia's shallow feeder roots and eventually breaks down to create the slightly acid soil on which they thrive. Overhead sprinklers provide deep irrigation, humidity in the air, and wash the dust and smog residue from the leaves.

Camellias grow on both sides of the statue and palm-lined North Vista.

*'Tabbs' surrounds the statue Arboriculture,
a youth holding the trunk of an apple tree.*

Flowers on **C. japonica**

All camellias belong to the genus *Camellia,* in the Theaceae, the tea family. In its natural state, the camellia is an evergreen tree that bears flowers in a single row of 5 to 9 petals, their color being white, pink, red, or yellow, depending on the species. The botanical classification of camellias divides the genus *Camellia* (which is a common name as well as a botanical name) into 200 species, most of which range naturally in a broad area of southeastern Asia.

The most commonly planted species in this country are *C. sasanqua, C. japonica,* and *C. reticulata.* Other introduced species have added new characteristics to garden camellias, such as the yellow flowers of *C. chrysantha,* the fragrance of *C. lutchuensis,* and the small leaves of *C. grijsii.*

In the gardens at the Huntington, the display labels include the genus name, *Camellia,* and the species name. The cultivar name is shown in single quotation marks—for example, *Camellia reticulata* 'Crimson Robe', or *Camellia sasanqua* 'Yuletide', or *Camellia japonica* 'Elegans Splendor'. Labels of hybrid camellias do not include the species name because hybrids are crosses between two species. For example, when a plant of the camellia species *lutchuensis* (a fragrant species with small leaves) was crossed or hybridized with *C. japonica* 'Tinsie' (a small flowered japonica cultivar), the result was a small leafed hybrid with fragrant flowers registered as *Camellia* 'Scented Gem' (located near the road in the North Canyon).

Examples of the single-flowered japonica species

Camellia sinensis *grows best in a moist climate. Hot, dry weather tends to crisp the edges of the leaves. In Southern California, tea is best planted as a curiosity. New seedlings better adapted to this climate have been introduced. Picture shows leaves, flower, and seed capsule.*

The seeds of **C. oleifera** *produce a high-grade oil that is used in cosmetics and in cooking in Japan and China.*

C. semiserrata

C. chrysantha *has small waxy gold yellow flowers often hidden in the large foliage of the plant. When word reached the west that there were camellia species in China with yellow flowers (more than 25 have been named to date), a rush was on to cross them with species like* C. japonica *that have large flowers. Unfortunately, hybrids with a strong yellow coloring have been very disappointing.*

C. granthamiana
*is sometimes called
the "fried egg"
camellia because of
its bright yellow
stamens surrounded
by stark white petals.*

C. grijsii.

ABOVE:
C. japonica *'Henry*
***E. Huntington'*,**
named after the
founder on the
occasion of the
institution's 75th
anniversary, was
released by Nuccio's
Nurseries in 1994.

BELOW:
Typical camellia label

Camellia japonica
'Henry E. Huntington'

Nuccio's Nurseries Introduction
1994   77680

In the wild, camellias that vary in some way from the species are called varieties or forms. However, in cultivation, a camellia that varies from its parents is called a cultivar (a contraction of the words "cultivated variety"). Wild varieties reproduce themselves through their seeds but cultivars need to be rooted or grafted in order to be duplicated. 'Scented Gem', described on page 15, is an example of a cultivar.

Some of the labels give historic information (country of origin and date introduced into the United States), others translate the Japanese or Chinese cultivar name into English, or indicate a "sport" (mutation) of its parent plant. Cultivars introduced at the Huntington are indicated on the label.

Hybrids (crosses between species) have produced some unusual results, such as *Camellia* 'Baby Bear', a cross between *C. rosaeflora* and *C. tsaii*, producing a dwarf, compact plant with miniature light pink flowers. *Camellia* 'Golden Glow' was an attempt to introduce yellow into a larger flower. One of its parents is *C. chrysantha*, a species with small waxy yellow flowers. The medium-sized flower of 'Golden Glow' is creamy white, deepening to light yellow at the base.

The cultivar name is limited only by the ingenuity of the originator. Foreign imports occasionally have retained their original titles, sometimes freely translated into English, but more often given new names.

LEFT: *'Baby Bear'*

RIGHT: *'Golden Glow'*

In earlier days, it was not uncommon for the same plant to have a different, localized name, which led to confusion in nomenclature. For example, 'Gigantea', introduced into the U. S. in the 1840s, was given many names, such as 'Mary Bell Glennan', 'Jolly Roger', and 'Gaiety', among others. At one point in time, it was exported back to Europe as 'Kilvintoniana'. Said to have been a seedling of 'Rubra Plena' in 1834, it also was given the name of 'Monstruoso Rubra'. This type of confusion continued over the years, as popular camellias were introduced from one place to another and given new names.

'Pink Perfection' was introduced into the United States in 1875 from Japan where it was called 'Usu-Otome' (pale maiden). Today, new cultivars in the United States are registered with the American Camellia Society, and this confusion in nomenclature has almost been eliminated.

Some plants are named to describe the flower: 'Pink Perfection', 'Freedom Bell', and 'Maroon and Gold'. Some glorify place names: 'Hawaii', 'Ville de Nantes', and 'Disneyland'. A great number are named after people, often national figures such as 'Richard Nixon', 'General Patton', 'Nancy Reagan', and many others. Most cultivars bearing personal names, however, are named after their originators or are named by the originators for their wives, members of their families, or close friends. Of course, there also are cultivars that just bear charming names for lovely blooms, such as 'Debutante', 'Spring Sonnet', 'Coral Delight', and 'Dazzler'.

'Gigantea'

C. japonica *'Gigantea'*, *introduced into the United States in the 1940s, has three flower forms that appear on the same tree. Anemone, pictured here, features a tuft of petaloids in the center. Other forms are semidouble and loose peony. The flowers are infected with a virus that produces white splotches, a dramatic contrast to the very dark green leaves. The spreading tree requires much space.*

'Freedom Bell'

'Maroon and Gold'

'Nancy Reagan'

'Coral Delight'

'Dazzler'

**C. wabisuke
'Sukiya'** *often
displays stamens with
few or no anthers.
A freshly picked
'Sukiya' is a favorite
flower in Japanese tea
ceremonies because
of its single flower
form. In this picture,
the fluted flower
would be chosen over
the more open one.*

T he cultivars of *Camellia japonica*, the most popular ornamental species, are dramatically different from the single flowered *C. japonica* typically found in nature. Over the hundreds of years this species has been in cultivation, some trees were discovered to be genetically unstable. For example, sometimes a branch would appear that produced a flower of a different form or color. Instead of being single, they had two or more rows of petals. Some had few or no stamens in the center. Others had margins or borders on the petals. If the flower was significantly different, this section of the branch would be cut from the main tree, rooted or grafted, and a new camellia tree would grow displaying the new flower form or color. This discovery would be given a new cultivar name. Thousands of cultivars of *C. japonica* have been "discovered" in this way.

When a branch shows a characteristic different from the rest of a camellia tree, it is called "sporting." As you walk through the gardens you will note occasionally a camellia branch that may be of a color, shape, or size different from the rest of the tree. Labels indicate when a cultivar is a "sport" of another named camellia.

Seven flower forms have been classified, making it easier to identify and describe them: single, semidouble, formal double, rose form double, anemone, loose peony, and full peony. The arrangement of petals dictates the form—from the single row of petals found in species camellias to numerous petal arrangements found in the flowers of many cultivars and sports.

Single

C. **Williams Lavender'** *was a hybrid produced in the United States in 1950. In England in the 1940s, some of the first* C. japonica *and* C. saluenensis *hybrid crosses were made by J.C. Williams and came to be known as Williamsii camellias.*

C. japonica *'Yamato-Nishiki' is probably
the best known Higo camellia in Japan.
Higos are characterized by their large show
of splayed stamens in the center and a
single row of petals (one usually much
smaller than the rest) in a nonsymmetrical
arrangement. This cultivar is white,
variegated pink and red. Higos are slow
growing and have compact growth, making
them good candidates for bonsai.*

Semi-double

C. 'Night Rider' *is a hybrid introduced from New Zealand. Very dark, almost black red camellias are unusual.*

'Grand Jury'

'Shishi-Gashira'

Formal
double

C. japonica 'Alba Plena Improved' *has darker green leaves, larger flowers, and is more vigorous than 'Alba Plena'. "Improved" usually means that the flower or some aspect of the plant is better than the original cultivar.*

Rose form double

C. hiemalis *'Interlude'* *is considered a*
formal double until the flower matures.
Then, a few stamens show in the
center, changing to rose form double.
It is also fragrant.

Anemone

C. japonica *William Penn* *was named
in 1954 but is rarely seen in gardens today.
It is a dark purple-red flower, marbled
white. The marbling, barely seen
in most flowers of this cultivar, is caused
by a virus intentionally introduced
to create variegation.*

'Tinsie Two'

'Elegans (Chandler)'

*Loose
peony*

Full peony

'Miss Tulare'

'Maculata Perfecta' *is an example of virus variegation of a camellia. Pictured in Ambroise Alexandre Verschaffelt,* Nouvelle Iconographie des Camellias *(Gand, 1849), 8e liv, Plate I.* *(Huntington Library: RB 274566)*

V ariegation of flowers occurs in two ways: either naturally or by intentionally introducing a virus to produce flowers with white blotches.

Natural variegation as a result of genetic instability creates flowers that are striped, speckled, or have a border. The pattern is evenly distributed throughout the flower and all flowers on the tree, although occasionally, you will see a very broad band of color on a flower or an entire petal of another color.

When a camellia is intentionally virused, the virus is introduced through a rootstock from a tree that is already virused. The virus then travels up through the graft, infecting the entire tree. Virused flowers are quite uneven in the distribution of white blotches, although when one sees a perfectly symmetrical distribution of white throughout a red flower, the effect is quite striking, as in the example of 'Adolphe Audusson Variegated'.

Variegation of flowers gives an added dimension to the color palette. Opinions differ about whether virusing injures the tree. To most observers, it does not. Occasionally, a virused tree may not have the vigor that it could have, but many factors play into the health and vigor of any plant.

C. japonica 'Adolphe Audusson Variegated' is an excellent example of virus variegation on a very dark red camellia. When the white is evenly distributed on a dark background, it is quite striking. Most people prefer the variegated form to the solid red. In most cases, the virus does not injure the tree.

39

'Anna Zucchini' is
an example of genetic
variegation and
sporting. Pictured in
Verschaffelt, October
1848, 10 liv., Plate I.
(Huntington
Library: RB 274566)

Anna Zucchini

Lith. de G. Jacqmain, Gand.

C. japonica *'Baronne de Bleichroeder',* an *old cultivar from Belgium (1878), is a rose form double. The crimson stripes are produced naturally, not by a virus. On the same tree appeared a sport with the same form* (PICTURED BELOW) *but in a solid color. This is very typical of camellias that are unstable, resulting in the introduction of many thousands of new cultivars over the centuries.*

'Choji Guruma'

here are many species of camellias, but the three most commonly planted in the United States—and the most popular—are *Camellia sasanqua*, *Camellia japonica*, and *Camellia reticulata*.

Sasanqua

A visitor to the gardens will find that the earliest species to bloom is *C. sasanqua*, which starts flowering in early fall and blooms into December. Recognized by its small evergreen leaves and its graceful form, *C. sasanqua* is extremely floriferous. Small flowers opening along the length of its branches present a dense mass of color, and many are fragrant. Sasanquas are often referred to as the "sun camellias" because they tolerate full sun in Southern California. Another characteristic of sasanquas is its flowers that shatter and fall to the ground, creating a colorful carpet.

Several specimens of *C. sasanqua* in the Huntington Botanical Gardens were planted in the early 1900s and have reached heights of fifteen to twenty feet. The collection of sasanquas at the Huntington is extensive, including most of the well-known cultivars. They can be seen in great profusion on "Sasanqua Hillside," along the eastern edge of the North Canyon, west of the Boone Gallery.

'Bonanza'

43

C. sasanqua
*'Double Rainbow'
flowers have an
attractive dark border.
Sasanqua petals are
not fused together as
are those of japonicas.
Here you see a petal
separating from the
rest of the flower.*

'Jean May'

C. sasanqua
'Snowfall' *is a*
startlingly white
camellia introduced
by Nuccio's Nurseries
in 1995. Many white
sasanquas are
semidouble or formal
double but this one
is single.

C. hiemalis
'Shishi-Gashira',
often mistaken for a
sasanqua, makes a
good ground cover,
especially for a slope
or to cover a large
area. It is low growing
to 2¹/₂ feet tall.

Japonica

The next species to bloom is the best known and most popular of all, *C. japonica*. More than one thousand are represented at the Huntington. The blooming season for this species is January to late March.

Greater selection in growth habits and in shape, size, and color of flower is found in *C. japonica* than in any other species of camellia. With dark glossy green leaves, *C. japonica* is a handsome garden specimen all year round, and when in bloom, few plants can match it for beauty of flower.

Nuccio's Nurseries Introductions

It is not possible in this small book to list the many cultivars of *C. japonica* in the Huntington Botanical Gardens, but a few plantings will be specifically mentioned. Nuccio's Nurseries of nearby Altadena, California, is world renowned for its camellia introductions. Most of their introductions since 1950 have been japonicas and close to one hundred of them are planted at the Huntington. Signage indicates the year of introduction.

C. japonica *'Guilio Nuccio'* *often produces rabbit ears (two are visible above) —petals that stand up instead of lying flat —a characteristic that is considered desirable on this cultivar. This is a Nuccio's Nurseries 1956 introduction.*

'Nuccio's Jewel'

C. japonica *ssp.* **rusticana**
*'Tsukamachi' is known as a snow
camellia because it grows in a snowy region
of Japan. Rusticanas have developed a few
characteristics that differ slightly from
japonicas, but not enough to be considered a
new species; hence they are a subspecies of*
C. japonica. *Many paintings in Japan
show a rusticana peeking out from
under the snow.*

The Huntington also has a collection of snow camellias, a subspecies of japonicas (botanically known as *C. japonica* ssp. *rusticana*) that has become acclimatized to a snowy region of Japan. The flowers are of medium size, in a range of colors, and the plant tends to have multiple lower branches that easily bend under the weight of snow. The rusticanas are located north of the Japanese house, midway along the central path lining the North Canyon.

Snow Camellias

Another special class of japonicas is known as Higo camellias. They were developed in Kumomoto, Japan, and can be identified by their single row of thick, round, broad petals surrounding a prominent display of yellow (sometimes red, pink, or white) stamens in the center. Their showy stamens are flared outwards in a way that brings to mind plum blossoms, another common name for these camellias. Cultivars with the highest stamen count are most valued. Plants are often grown in pots and pruned into bonsai shapes.

Higos

LEFT: *'Azuma Nishiki'*

RIGHT: **Higo** *flower buds are rounded.*

'Elegans (Chandler)' pictured
*in Verschaffelt, 1848,
12 liv., Plate II.
(Huntington
Library: RB 274566)*

BELOW LEFT:
*'Elegans
(Chandler)'*

BELOW RIGHT:
'Elegans Miniata'

In 1831, an English nurseryman named Alfred Chandler discovered a camellia from a number of seedlings he had grown from the seeds of a camellia named 'Waratah'. This camellia produced some of the best genetic sports still available today. Descendants of the original 'Elegans (Chandler)', a rose pink anemone form, have appeared variegated ('Elegans Miniata'), light pink edged white ('Elegans Splendor'), and white ('Elegans Champagne'), in sizes larger and smaller, as a full peony form, and with fimbriated petals. Registered sports are displayed on Elegans Lane, located west of the North Vista lawn, and are excellent illustrations of the genetic instability of camellias. The thirteen sports of 'Elegans' not only are distinct from one another, but all have good growth habits, making them desirable plants for the home garden.

LEFT: *'Elegans Splendor'*

RIGHT: *'Elegans Champagne'*

53

Reticulata

The species that blooms latest in the season, from mid-February to late March, is *C. reticulata*, considered by many the most spectacular of all. Tall, rather open shrubs with large, dull, green leaves, they bear a profusion of enormous blooms, many up to seven inches in diameter, with high, fluted petals. Most of the flower forms are either semidouble or loose peony, ranging in color from pink and orchid pink to red and red-marbled white. Many have an almost iridescent quality. Since the plant itself is very open with comparatively few branches and leaves, the flowers stand out in truly dramatic fashion.

A camellia that did not look like a *C. japonica* was brought to England from China in an East India Company ship, commanded by Captain Richard Rawes, in 1820. Although spindly and unprepossessing in appearance, it was lovingly cared for by Thomas Carey Palmer, of Bromley, Kent. A full six years passed before it produced its first bloom — a rose-crimson, semidouble flower of startling beauty. The plant was named after Captain Rawes and is still available in the trade. Later, it was considered a *C. reticulata*, although many years passed before it was re-identified as a hybrid reticulata. To all appearances, it carries the characteristics of its reticulata parent: large, leathery leaves, a lanky form, and large flowers that bloom late in the season.

'Captain Rawes'

2784.

'Captain Rawes'
was shown in
Curtis's Botanical
Magazine *(#2784)*
with its carmine rose
red semidouble
irregular petals.
Compare this 1827
illustration with the
photograph of the
flower opposite.

C. reticulata
'Professor Tsai'
was named after the
Chinese professor who
assisted with the
release of the first
reticulata camellias
to the United States.

An interesting story surrounds the arrival of these beautiful flowers in the United States. Although they were admired, they were for many years simply thought of as curiosities, and their appeal was limited. It was not until the 1930s that news of forms of *C. reticulata*, growing in Yunnan Province in China, reached American camellia growers. Dr. Walter E. Lammerts, then in charge of research at Descanso Gardens, entered into correspondence with Professor H. T. Tsai of the Kunming Botanic Garden in Yunnan, who confirmed the existence of these plants. He reported that twenty cultivars were to be found in the province. Arrangements were made to have a complete set of the plants flown to California, and in 1948 the first shipment arrived in San Francisco. At about the same time, although working independently, the late Ralph S. Peer, in conjunction with the Southern California Camellia Society, also had contacted Professor Tsai and arranged for specimens of *C. reticulata* to be sent to the Huntington for testing and propagation.

Many difficulties arose when the plants finally arrived. Although they stood the long trip to this country fairly well, the U.S. Department of Agriculture insisted that they be barerooted and fumigated before being released. Several of the plants could not withstand the rough treatment. Nurserymen then discovered that they were very difficult to propagate and many of the original specimens were lost. Fortunately, it was still possible to obtain a few additional shipments from China, but political conditions soon shut off that supply. By pooling the results of work at

'Mouchang'

Descanso and the Huntington, many of the original twenty varieties were established. The introduction of what came to be known as the "Yunnan reticulatas" was a major horticultural achievement and opened a new field in camellia culture.

The reticulatas, representative of those early arrivals from China, are located at the northwest corner of the North Vista in an area labeled as Reticulata Knoll. They have a display label of a different color from the others. Although reticulatas are difficult to propagate, when once established, they grow with amazing vigor and rapidity. 'Shot Silk' and 'Captain Rawes' in the North Vista are both more than twenty feet tall.

Near Reticulata Knoll is a planting of *C. reticulata* 'William Hertrich' (Henry Huntington's superintendent of the gardens and author of the 1954 three-volume series *Camellias in the Huntington Gardens*), which bears deep cherry-red semidouble flowers on a nicely shaped tree.

A great deal of hybridizing has been done using *C. reticulata* as a parent. Some hybrids have been spectacular; a few include: 'Howard Asper', 'Francie L.', 'Donation', and 'Carl Tourje'—the latter produced at the Huntington.

'William Hertrich'

'Purple Gown'

C. reticulata *'Lila Naff'* has, like most reticulatas, flowers, buds, seeds, and leaves that are larger than japonicas. It is described as a silver pink, semidouble flower with wide petals.

C. 'Scented Sun' is white with an occasional pink stripe but often has branches of flowers in shades of pink. This hybrid captured the large size of one parent and the fragrance of another.

n addition to creating beautiful blooms, horticulturists experiment with hybrids for many reasons. It is always hoped that a cross may develop a plant that combines the best features of both parents—lovely flowers with a graceful plant, for example. Experiments also are being conducted to produce camellias that will resist sun, heat, or cold, thus enlarging the areas where they may be cultivated. The dream of every camellia grower is to produce a large yellow flower. Several camellias of cream color with hints of yellow are making their way into the trade. Many new hybrid introductions have fragrance. By crossing a large japonica flower, for example, with a species flower that carries fragrance, a larger flower with fragrance might be produced. (See 'Scented Sun' opposite)

Many *C. saluenensis* crosses have produced some interesting results. The Huntington introduction, *C.* 'Beverly L. Baylies' (BELOW LEFT), for example, has a profusion of flower buds, all opening to produce a long blooming season. The upright tree with full foliage makes a good landscape plant.

The Huntington has introduced some choice camellias over the years. One cultivar, *C. japonica* 'Little Michael', was named for the son of Rudy Moore, curator of the camellia collections for twenty years. The miniature anemone flower is soft pink with creamy white petaloids in its center. This introduction is an example of combining two desirable qualities—a tree with a compact growth habit and an unusually delightful flower.

Hybrids and Huntington Introductions

LEFT:
'Beverly L. Baylies'

RIGHT:
'Little Michael'

C. japonica *'Betty's Beauty'* *is one of
more than fifteen sports from the 'Betty
Sheffield' line. Introduced by the
Huntington in 1975, it is a stable camellia
whose flowers come "true" and will not
revert to a solid color.*

C. japonica *'Rudy's Magnoliaeflora'* *is*
a sport of 'Magnoliaeflora', an old camellia
that arrived in Italy from Japan in 1886.
The blush pink cup-shaped flower was
called 'Hagoromo' in Japan. Rudy Moore,
curator of the Huntington camellia
collection, discovered the sport and gave it its
name in 1988. Its color is a deeper pink
than the original.

'Elena Nobile'

C amellias are easy to grow. A small amount of care and attention will produce a maximum of attractive plants and flowers. Unlike roses, they are not prey for most insects; aphids, caterpillars, and grasshoppers seldom damage camellia plants.

One of the few diseases to which camellias are susceptible is petal blight, a fungus that is difficult to control. The best course of action to keep the disease from doing too much damage is to be conscientious about picking up and destroying dropped flowers. There is no efficient chemical control.

Some camellias, particularly *C. sasanqua* and *C. reticulata* cultivars, sometimes get a canker disease that attacks the trunks and branches of the trees. If this appears, the best remedy is to do as little pruning as possible, as the disease enters from wounds. Overhead watering can create humid conditions favorable for the disease to grow. If a tree is vigorous, it can stay ahead of the fungal growth. A healthy tree can stop the canker from progressing.

Red spider mites will find their way to the underneath parts of the newly formed leaves in hot and dry weather, especially in Southern California. Rarely do spider mites destroy a camellia. What you may see is a speckling on the leaves that takes on a dull green or bronze shade. An alternative to chemical sprays would be to spray the leaves on the undersides with water under high pressure.

TOP LEFT: Petal blight is a fungus that turns a beautiful flower into brown mush. This photo shows the progress of the disease from small brown specks into larger areas, until the unsightly flower drops to the ground.

TOP RIGHT: Canker disease can attack *C. sasanqua* and *C. reticulata* more severely than *C. japonica*. The fungus appears to enter a branch that has been wounded or pruned and the canker can move onto the trunk.

BOTTOM LEFT: Aphids are soft bodied small insects that attack only newly emerged leaves in the spring. Old camellia leaves are too tough for them to insert their sucking mouth parts. You will often see aphids clustered at the tips of the branches in the spring along with a number of ants (the ants do no harm to camellias).

BOTTOM RIGHT: Sometimes during a sudden hot and dry spell, when camellias have not been well watered, the leaves will become scorched, as shown in this photo. The discoloration is usually in the center of the leaf and the tissue is brown in the center.

Camellias are propagated in three ways: by seed, by cuttings, and by grafting. Several books and pamphlets describe these methods in detail, and any camellia enthusiast will go out of his or her way to show you how to grow seeds and start cuttings, or guide your hand through the intricacies of camellia grafting.

The successful hobbyist may wish to go still further by joining a camellia society and entering blooms in the various shows. All camellia growing areas have local societies; the American Camellia Society, Massee Lane Gardens, 100 Massee Lane, Fort Valley, Georgia 31030 has members throughout the camellia growing world. Their web site address is: http://www.peach.public.lib.ga.us/ACS/ and e-mail is acs@alltel.net. California has several camellia societies scattered from San Diego to Sacramento. Camellia shows usually start in January or February and are held on succeeding weekends, beginning in San Diego and working northward from January through March. Contact the Southern California Camellia Society for show dates. (See SOURCES)

For those who already know camellias, we hope that a tour through the Huntington Botanical Gardens will be an occasion for renewing old friendships and for making new ones among the more recently developed cultivars. To the fledgling grower, you now can see intriguing possibilities for your own camellias. Enjoy the gardens, consult books from the following bibliography—then "plant" your new knowledge! ❧

LEFT: *Reticulata seed capsules are large and brown.*

RIGHT: *Japonica capsules look like miniature apples with a blush on the side facing the sun.*

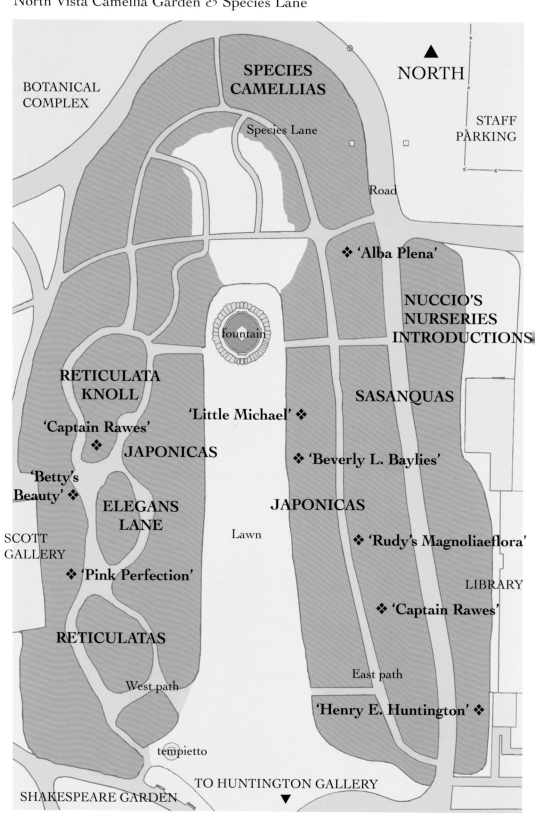

SPECIES
CAMELLIAS

NORTH

BOTANICAL
COMPLEX

Species Lane

STAFF
PARKING

Road

❖ 'Alba Plena'

NUCCIO'S
NURSERIES
INTRODUCTIONS

fountain

RETICULATA
KNOLL

SASANQUAS

'Little Michael' ❖

'Captain Rawes'
❖

JAPONICAS

❖ 'Beverly L. Baylies'

'Betty's
Beauty' ❖

ELEGANS
LANE

JAPONICAS

SCOTT
GALLERY

Lawn

❖ 'Rudy's Magnoliaeflora'

❖ 'Pink Perfection'

LIBRARY

❖ 'Captain Rawes'

RETICULATAS

East path

West path

'Henry E. Huntington' ❖

tempietto

TO HUNTINGTON GALLERY

SHAKESPEARE GARDEN

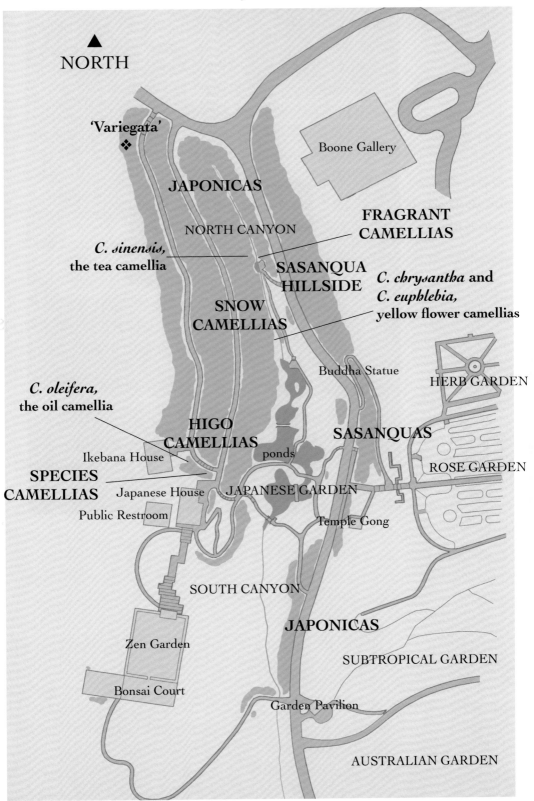

▲
NORTH

'Variegata' ❖

JAPONICAS

Boone Gallery

NORTH CANYON

FRAGRANT
CAMELLIAS

C. sinensis,
the tea camellia

SASANQUA
HILLSIDE

C. chrysantha and
C. euphlebia,
yellow flower camellias

SNOW
CAMELLIAS

Buddha Statue

HERB GARDEN

C. oleifera,
the oil camellia

HIGO
CAMELLIAS

ponds

SASANQUAS

Ikebana House

SPECIES
CAMELLIAS

Japanese House

JAPANESE GARDEN

ROSE GARDEN

Public Restroom

Temple Gong

SOUTH CANYON

JAPONICAS

Zen Garden

SUBTROPICAL GARDEN

Bonsai Court

Garden Pavilion

AUSTRALIAN GARDEN

*'Francie L.' and
lion marble chair*

Selective Bibliography and Camellia Sources

Books

Dunmire, John R., editor. *Azaleas, Rhododendrons and Camellias*, 2nd ed., Menlo Park, CA: Sunset Books/ Sunset Publishing Corporation, 1999.

Durrant, Tom. *The Camellia Story*. Auckland: Heinemann Publishers, 1982. Out of print. Good if you can get your hands on one.

Galle, Fred P. and Michael D. Smith, editors. *All About Azaleas, Camellias & Rhododendrons*. San Ramon, CA: Ortho Books, 1995.

Gonos, Arthur A., editor. *Camellia Nomenclature*. 23rd rev. ed. The Southern California Camellia Society, Inc., 1999. A descriptive list of all cultivars of camellias now being grown in the western world and especially the United States. A must for anyone interested in growing and exhibiting camellias in flower shows. Available from the Southern California Camellia Society.

Hertrich, William. *Camellias in the Huntington Gardens: observations on their culture and behavior and descriptions of cultivars*. 3 vols. San Marino, CA: Huntington Botanical Gardens, 1954–1958. Out of print. Garden supervisor Hertrich photographed and described camellias in the Gardens.

Hung Ta, Chang. *Camellias*. Portland, OR: Timber Press, Inc., 1984. Out of print. Good botanical line drawings and descriptions of camellias.

Macoboy, Stirling. *The Illustrated Encyclopedia of Camellias*. Portland, OR: Timber Press, Inc., 1998. The best current, available, in-depth book on camellias. Many illustrations and good text.

Rolfe, Jim. *Gardening with Camellias: a New Zealand Guide*. Auckland: Godwit Press Limited, 1992. Out of print. Good general text and photos.

Savige, Thomas J., comp. *The International Camellia Register*. 2 vols. Australia : International Camellia Society,

*C. japonica **'Margarete Hertrich'**, named in 1944 for the wife of Huntington superintendent, William Hertrich, was discovered among many hundreds of seedlings planted on the grounds. Most seedlings do not have flowers worthy of being registered and instead become rootstock for grafting camellias.*

1993. Reference text for researchers, hybridizers, growers, and hobbyists. Lists nomenclature, history, descriptions of camellias historical to modern.

Trehane, David. A *Plantsman's Guide to Camellias*. London: Ward Lock Limited, 1990. Out of print. A concise guide to camellias based on climate in the British Isles. Not enough details for the specialist.

Camellia Nursery

Nuccio's Nurseries, 3555 Chaney Trail, Altadena, CA 91001. Telephone (626) 794-3383. In business 66 years and internationally known, Nuccio's is a wholesale/retail nursery specializing in camellias and azaleas. Mail orders, free catalog. Sells scions, usually January through March.

Check with your local nursery for sources of cultivars of camellias in your area.

Periodicals

The Camellia Journal, published by the American Camellia Society, 100 Massee Lane, Fort Valley, Georgia 31030. Small, chatty quarterly.

Yearbook, published by the American Camellia Society (see above). Yearly publication lists awards and articles.

The Camellia Review, four issues a year published by The Southern California Camellia Society, 7475 Brydon Road, La Verne, CA 91750. Camellia hobbyist news and trophy winner announcements.

International Camellia Journal, published annually by the International Camellia Society. Articles on research, history, trials, and travels relating to camellias.

Societies

The American Camellia Society (address above). Telephone: (912) 967-2358. Membership includes *The Camellia Journal* and the annual *Yearbook*.

International Camellia Society, United States, Mrs. Anabelle Fetterman, P.O. Box 306, Clinton, NC 28328. Membership includes *International Camellia Journal* and opportunities to travel to International Congress meetings every two years in a different country.

Peninsula Camellia Society, Membership, Franklin H. Olmsted, Treasurer, 240 W. Charleston Rd., Palo Alto, CA 94306.

The Southern California Camellia Society (address under "Periodicals").
   Membership includes announcements of monthly meetings and camellia shows and *The Camellia Review*.

Other Resources

American Classic Tea, 6617 Maybank Highway, Wadmalaw Island, SC 29487. Phone: (800) 443-5987. Email: chastea@awod.com.
   The Charleston Tea Plantation in South Carolina is North America's only tea plantation. Their catalog is a source for their tea and tea-related products, including an educational video on tea harvesting and processing in North America.